Journey of a Dream

Darlene Carter

always follow your dreams

Journey of a Dream Press

First printing in 2004 (Doggie in the Window Publications)
Second edition 2018 (Journey of a Dream Press)

This book was printed in the United States of America.

For permission to reproduce selections from this book or to order additional copies, contact:

Journey of a Dream Presss
2888 Winchester Court
Duluth GA 30096

Website: www.journeyofadreamcom

Email: Journeyofadream@comcast.net

ISBN 978-0-9749876-0-6

Acknowledgements

xpressions of gratitude and acknowledgements are distributed throughout this book as it seems appropriate to link specific poems to their source of inspiration. However, there are some thanks that warrant special notice as this dream would never have been realized without the influence and support of these individuals.

I am grateful for the love and support of my wonderful family. My husband, Tom, is also my best friend and greatest supporter. The journey would have been very lonely without him.

Nancy Lane recognized a spark of creativity in me before I was willing or able to acknowledge the possibility. She nurtured and encouraged that spark until I was strong enough to own it. I can never thank Nancy enough for her part in the realization of this dream and for the healing I've experienced in my life since we met. I look forward to continuing the journey with this Mighty Companion.

Fran Stewart, author of <u>Orange as Marmalade</u>, has supported me tirelessly with her editing skills and insights. Fran is my weekly MasterMind partner and she has held the vision of this book as a reality from conception to birth. I am grateful for her support and friendship.

Special thanks to my Breath Coach, John Cenni, for providing a safe place for me to identify and resolve the emotional blocks to completing this book.

I am grateful for the love and support of the Atlanta Breathworkers' Community. You have touched my heart and inspired me with your stories of healing and courage. Your willingness to help others discover their strengths and realize their dreams has been a blessing in my life.

Contents

*A*wareness

*A*cceptance

*A*ction . . .

It was a bit of a shock to realize I am not a particularly "religious" person, but I am striving to be more spiritually in tune.

I lost faith in my religion and am now beginning to realize that maybe I expected too much without a lot of effort on my part . . . blaming others for my disappointments. Even when religion offers me comfort and guidance, I must accept that my fellow members are human beings and they have their lessons to learn. They are not perfect and neither am I . . . Why should I demand perfection? God doesn't! We are all perfectly imperfect human beings.

I no longer receive comfort or guidance from the traditions of my childhood religion; however, I am learning to trust in my own spirituality and in God. This requires faith and action, and I am ready for both!

Part I

ALONG
FAITH'S
PATHWAY

Write it on a cloud,
    Watch it float away.
        Cast away your doubts,
            Begin anew each day.

This piece was written for Nancy Lane, my massage therapist, my friend, and my Mighty Companion. Nancy was my first great teacher, and she taught me not only how to heal my body but my spiritual wounds as well.

Years ago Nancy asked me a very simple but powerful question as she was massaging the sore and tightened muscles in my frozen shoulder.

"How's your spiritual life, Darlene?"

It was a question that changed my life literally and forever.

My spiritual life is wonderful, Nancy, and getting better every day.

My Guardian Angel

I thought my wing was broken.

You knew it was only wounded.

I felt my spirit was shattered.

You had faith it could be healed.

Thank you for being my guardian angel

And for helping me remember that

The dark days only come along

So we can fully appreciate

The beautiful bright ones.

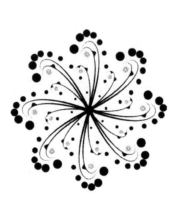

Whirlwind of Love

I stand in the midst of a whirlwind,
A myriad of emotions passing by.

Today I pull anger from the passing array
And examine its pulse and texture
Until I allow it to bubble to the surface,
And feel the red, hot energy as never before.

I allow myself to be angry.
I give me permission to be mad.
To feel the hate and resentment
As it demands to be felt.

For feeling is releasing;
And releasing is loving.
And that is my goal . . .
To stand in the midst of a whirlwind
And be surrounded only by love.

It rained the day after my dream disintegrated, and I spent the entire day in bed. I cried as I grieved the passing of a lifelong dream. I curled into a ball and sobbed tears that needed release. I let the dream fall away. I kissed it tenderly and caressed it and let it have its freedom. Realizing that I alone hold the truth for me was both powerful and painful. No mighty hero would arrive on a great steed risking everything to save me.

I alone know what is right for me. Pain, once acknowledged and felt, can be healed, and I began to realize that I can be my own hero. I hold the keys that dissolve the bars on my prison. I walk freely down the path of my choosing . . . no longer waiting to be rescued by a source outside myself.

I am free to create a new dream!

Releasing a Dream

The Universe cried with me today
And the rain was a balm
To my wounded heart.

Today I wrapped myself
In a cocoon of grief
As I mourned the loss of a dream.

The sun will return.
The clouds will dance again,
My heart will be mended.

Tomorrow a new dream will replace the old;
But today is a day to weep
And acknowledge the pain.

Forgiveness is the key to the prison I constructed to hold my doubts and fears. Guilt is an emotion exclusive to humans. No other animal on the planet experiences it.

When I harbor guilty thoughts about myself, I sometimes need help in finding a way to let it go. Guilt is toxic to my body and serves no other purpose except to stifle my dreams and hold me back from realizing my full potential.

Forgiveness of self is the first step to peace.

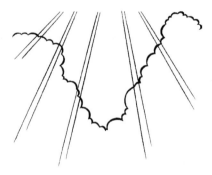

Forgiveness

Throw off the sodden blanket
Of guilt and remorse.

Embrace the luscious velvet
Of forgiveness.

Forgive yourself.

God already has!

I am a breath coach. I teach clients a conscious, connected breathing technique to relieve stress and create more peace in their lives. I heard someone refer to the hopelessness of fear as a 'band of steel' around her heart, and it touched a cord in mine. I have felt that steel and I know how heavy and constricting it can be. Finding the courage to allow it to dissolve is a wondrous thing.

Band of Steel

A black band of steel circled my heart
Obscuring all love and compassion.
I thought it protected,
Saved me from hurt.
I felt I would die if it left me.

My heart knew better
And summoned the breath
To make way for truth and compassion.
For the black band of steel
Was nothing but fear
Dissolved by the tears of forgiveness.

Of all the wonderful things we can do for ourselves and others, there is no greater gift we can give than to deal with our own pain. When we find it in our hearts to forgive ourselves or someone else, we have lightened the load of the world and contributed to peace.

If you just thought of someone with whom you are angry or disappointed, maybe it's time to explore those feelings and consider the option of forgiveness.

Healing

Today I did something
For the Universe;
Something wonderful,
Loving and free.

Today I did something
For the Universe . . .
I healed an old hurt
Inside of me.

After a long walk on the beach I began to see, really see, each person coming toward me. As their very different and unique needs gradually became clear to me, I began to offer a silent blessing to each of them. A need for peace for one; a need for acceptance for another, and so on until I felt overwhelmed by the sheer volume of the needs.

It seemed as though thousands of people had materalized on the sands at the water's edge, and I understood the message being offered to me. If I could empathize and understand the needs of these strangers, how much easier it would be to simply focus within myself and recognize my own need for healing and claim my own blessing. Trying to heal others is exhausting and impossible. Healing oneself is the only hope there is.

Needs

Be not distracted
By the multitudes;
For their needs are many
And overwhelming.

Focus within,
Heal yourself;
And the world
Will heal around you.

Once, as I neared a grove of cypress trees, an irrational fear was sudden and powerful. I felt faint and paused, afraid to take another step even though I knew consciously that in the present moment I was in a safe place. There was no danger here. This fear was from deep within and long ago, its cause a mystery which was ready to reveal itself for release.

I had come here with a trusted companion to lie on the ground in this circle of trees and breathe in the presence of their healing energy. As I lay on the soft bed of pine straw and smelled their unmistakable odor, the memories came flooding back along with the emotions which had been suppressed for so long...childhood emotions of shame, anger and fear.

As I breathed and cried, I allowed the balancing energy of these grand old trees to cradle me, and I knew again the peace and power of letting go.

Enter the fear.

Feel its power.

Embrace its source,

And know your own strength.

Mountaintop

I stand on the mountaintop
Alone and unguarded.
Vulnerable
Unsafe
Without armor or shield.

I lift my hands toward heaven
And shout aloud
The truth.
Secrets
Released into the universe.

No longer a weight on my heart or my soul.
I feel the very breath of God
As He whispers to me,
"Well done, my child, your spirit is free!"

People who spark my anger or annoy me the most have often turned out to be my greatest teachers. As soon as I become willing to 'own' my anger, resentment, or jealousy I begin to see the situation or person in a different light. It is the start of my own healing. When I 'get it' the other person either moves out of my life or suddenly seems to have a new 'attitude'. In actual fact, it is always about me and something I need to learn about myself.

Reflections

I am uncomfortable with your fear
Because it validates mine.
I am annoyed by your anger
     Because mine lurks
     Just beneath the surface.
I think "if only" you were
More serene
More in control
More like me.
Then I realize
You <u>are</u> me.
We are children of God together
You are my mirror.
If I choose,
I can see only innocence
     Reflected there.

*I found myself in the presence of a loved one who was very angry with me. Gradually I became aware that I was no longer responding defensively or with fear. I celebrate the decision to own **my** emotions and release the habit of simply reacting to the emotions of others.*

I am no longer frightened by someone who is feeling their emotions for I am fully aware of my own.

Permission

I give you permission to be angry,
To be unhappy,
 mean,
 confused.

I give you permission to be angry,
Without permission to take me there too.

Feelings, feelings, feelings. In the past I considered feelings another "F" word, something to be avoided as frightening and vulnerable.

The unexpected death of my Dad when I was four years old planted the seed for development of a lifelong talent of dissociating or hiding from my feelings. Over the years, I've learned that disallowing feelings only means that energy gets stuffed and collected in the physical body. It ferments and festers until some future event triggers its demand to be felt. To deny this last cry for release leaves the welcome mat out for disease to manifest in a body weakend by the weight of the past.

Today I am grateful for the courage to feel my feelings and heal old wounds. I am happy and healthy as I stand in the moment that is now.

Power of the Present

Unresolved feelings from the past
Are dragged into the present,
Tethered to the physical body
Like a ball and chain.

Any link dissolved through feeling and release
Weakens the bondage to the past,
Moving me closer to the day
I will stand forever in the power of the present

As I release the past,
I find freedom in today.

Sharing a friend's pain because of the death of her grandmother allowed me to re-connect with the same painful loss. I was ill when my grandmother died. I was recovering from surgery and was weakened by anemia. I simply wasn't able to fully feel the pain of losing someone I loved so much. It wasn't until I held my friend and helped mourn her loss that I realized I had my own unexpressed grief.

We honor our loved ones by feeling and expressing our grief at their passing, not by holding onto it and allowing it to restrict or affect our lives. My grandmother was a strong, loving person and I miss her. I smile when I think of her now because the grief is behind me. Ahead is a chance to celebrate her life and legacy of love.

Pain

I have touched your pain
And my soul weeps;
I have touched your pain
And found it raw and familiar.

Inside your sorrow
Lies my own untouched grief,
And in feeling your pain
I have connected with my own.

Now my burden is lighter
And my heart is freer,
Simply because
I have touched your pain.

Someone was unkind to me today and accused me of being unkind to her. It frightened and hurt me. My first reaction was to explain, excuse, defend, and deny. However, I saw the pain in her eyes and realized whatever my intent had been, the unkindness was real to her. I told her it hadn't been my intent to be rude, and I was sorry if it seemed that I had. I still felt angry and weak for not defending myself.

Tonight I was reminded by a friend that it takes courage to be kind when someone isn't being kind in return. I realized I had a choice . . . I could release the anger and hurt to be at peace or hold onto something that would be forever toxic in my body. I chose peace and pray that I will always have the courage to be kind in any situation.

Courage to be Kind

It's easy to return a kindness
When our hearts are full
From the kindness of a stranger
Or a loved one.

It takes courage to be kind
In a world filled with fear.
It takes courage to be kind
When we feel threatened or hurt.

We have the power to change the world
When we pray for courage to be kind
When someone else isn't.

Sitting on the beach today I have chosen peace. Watching the waves coming and going reminds me that there is Divine Order in everything. I only have to quieten my mind, listen, and be willing to feel the emotions needing to be felt.

I could have chosen panic and despair this morning instead of peace because the circumstances surrounding me today are sad and frightening. I recently learned my brother-in-law has prostate cancer. My first reaction was one of shock, fear, and sadness. I thought of returning home early to be with my family but felt I was here for a reason, maybe to learn something about myself.

Then God sent His miracle. A long distance phone call from a friend who hadn't called in over a year reminded me that God always provides what is needed in a perfect way and with perfect timing. My friend's brother-in-law recently underwent surgery for prostate cancer, and he is doing very well, looking forward to a full recovery. I had been on her mind all day and she had a feeling she needed to call me. After our conversation I remembered I was "at choice" in this situation. I decided to choose HOPE, and in hope there is peace.

Choice

All is right in the world.
Peace is possible in every heart,
I am always at choice;
Every moment is golden
Offering me a chance for

Growth
Peace
Learning
Understanding
Healing
Releasing
Feeling

The choice is mine.
What will I choose today?

For my son, Tommy, who loves the beach as much, or more, than I do. Our hearts beat to the same rhythm and I am grateful for his love and support in my life.

On the Beach

On the beach I become a refugee
From fear and confusion.
I sit alone with myself and God
Watching the waves
Curling toward me.
Their constant motion,
Their gentle rhythm
Soothe me.
I realize the sound is a melody
My heart had forgotten.

or Leo, who never let fear of failure stop his forward progress. Thank you for recognizing my ability to handle my human errors with grace. You provided a safe place for me to learn this lesson and I am grateful.

Lessons

Celebrate your victories
While seeking to understand your defeats.
For it is through studying
The face of our failures
That we learn life's most important lessons,
And achieve goals thought impossible.

Fear not the failures,
But the waste of doing nothing.

Part II

The Spirit
Of a
Child

He who wounds
    The spirit of a child
        Owes an awesome debt
            Whose currency is tears.

We are all children of God. We have a childlike spirit inside us which nourishes the part of us that is linked to the Holy Father. The Spirit of a Child lives in each of us. We only have to be sure we don't push it into hiding. Anger, greed, lust, envy, and fear drive our spirits into hiding and threaten to bankrupt the universe.

No matter how old I am or how damaged I might feel, somewhere inside me lives the Spirit of a Child. Make a safe place in your heart for your child to play, and God will reward you with blessings you cannot imagine.

The most powerful fear I have ever felt is the fear of being afraid. Fear occurs at all age levels but it is seldom more appalling than when it is manifested in the life of a child. No real or imagined circumstance has ever produced the level of paralysis or pain that endures from avoiding life out of fear of being hurt. "Fear of fear" is an endless circle of grief that can become a way of life. It is only resolved by facing that which is feared and feeling the emotions.

The celebration of life that follows that kind of release is what gives our lives here on earth a divine purpose and allows each of us to recognize our individual gifts and talents.

Despair

The saddest sight in the universe
Is despair in the eyes of a child;
Innocence plunged into a deep abyss
From which there seems no escape.

As hope becomes alien and out of reach,
It is as though time has been suspended.
Fear deepens and assumes control . . .
A life out of balance becomes the norm.

Time With A Child

To see through a child's eye
Is to experience the wonder
Of everything new.

I'll take a moment today
To spend time with a child
And experience the joy of innocence.

Sometimes that child
Is simply the one
Who lives inside of me.

This was written on Mother's Day. Early that morning as I sat in my swing looking over a backyard that usually has more "weeds" than cultivated vegetation, I realized I wasn't writing just about flowers.

As I jotted down notes and this poem took shape, I was reminded of children and the many different circumstances in which they grow up. Some are born into loving, nurturing families, while others find themselves in very harsh and cold circumstances with little or no guidance or support. But like the strong and determined weeds that find ways to bloom even in the most challenging environments, many of these children become success stories and inspirations of perserverance.

The next time you pluck that lone dandelion from your immaculate lawn, take a minute and really look at it and admire its effortless beauty. The next time you have an opportunity to interact with a child, yours or someone else's, take a moment to really see and appreciate their potential. Seeing it reflected in your eyes just might spark a miracle they will remember for a lifetime.

Weeds

Enjoy the weeds
For they, too, have value.

Not planted in neat or graceful rows,
Nor nurtured by loving and gentle hands,
But sprouting, unwanted and boastful,
In places as varied as they.

The delicate beauty of a dandelion
Or the fragrant perfume of the honeysuckle,
Each in its own unique way
Offers us a slice of God's love
Found no where else.

So, be still, and enjoy the weeds
And the lessons of love they offer.

I *haven't written anything dark in a long time. I consider this piece one of those, a reminder of a time when I fled from my emotions, especially the fear. I was somewhat disturbed to find these words flowing onto the paper in the early morning hours. It took a few days before I was willing to refine the thoughts and print them. I believe I have learned to face my fears rather than run from them and do not like being reminded of that old habit of hiding.*

This process, however, has helped me realize that I cannot be defined in terms of black or white . . . good or evil. I am all or I am nothing. I acknowledge and celebrate the parts of me that I called dark, sad or frightened as well as those parts of me that are light, happy and carefree, courageous and bold. Without the contrast how can I appreciate either, how can I be the perfectly imperfect human that I am?

When I find myself facing a new fear, or an old one, and realize I just want to float away and hide, I give myself permission to do just that . . . without guilt or shame. In all things there is perfect timing. I choose to honor my ability to know when the time is right to face and release yet another fear and move on to the next part of the adventure.

Hiding

As I float above a sea of emotions,
I drift down and see myself
Small
Alone
Frightened.
I feel the fear
I'm shocked by its power,
Terrified it is real.

Quickly I adjust my altitude
Up, up, back to the safe place
Where I hide
From the fear,
From the pain,
But mostly
From myself.

The birth of my daughter Stephanie was a gift from God, an unexpected miracle. Watching the beauty of her life unfold inspires me. I'm reminded that when things don't go according to my plan it's often because God has a better one.

A Rosebud

I am a tiny rosebud
Growing wild in the forest or field.
Soft delicate petals clasp tightly
The tender core of my soul.

Each morning I look to the heavens
To receive what God has provided.
Sometimes sunshine warms my heart,
Often raindrops cleanse and feed me.

With gratitude I drink it all in,
The rain and the wind
The thunder and the sunlight,
Knowing I am nourished by each.

Gradually I begin to open my heart,
Relaxing the layers of protection.
In safety and love I release my grip,
And extend my beauty for all to see.

                I am
                a tiny
                rosebud
                on a journey
                        to become
                                the Rose.

When my daughter was very young she accidentally broke a vase and I reacted with anger and blame. It was a momentary opportunity for me to vent my own suppressed anger which had absolutely nothing to do with the broken vase or my daughter. She was punished and the incident was forgotten, at least it was forgotten by me.

Many years later in a very emotional family therapy session she shared her feelings about the incident, and I realized it was as real for her in the telling as the day it happened. My reaction to the broken vase was proof to her that I cared more about a small piece of glass than about her. She had been carrying that moment and its toxic consequences for years, using it as evidence to support a feeling of not being loved.

Each moment in our lives is precious and unique. Each moment offers an opportunity for learning. I learned to be mindful of the impact my actions have on others, and I learned to hug my children and tell them I love them more often than I scold them.

A golden moment

Suspended in time

Might last only a minute

Or a lifetime.

For my daughter, Kathy, who inspires and amazes me. On this day she made a commitment to God and the joy in her voice was evident when she called to tell me she would be baptized on Christmas Eve. How wonderful.

While the decision had been formulating in her mind for sometime, she had planned to step forward at a time when circumstances would be perfect for her to stand before the large congregation and announce her decision to join the church. As often happens when we open our hearts and minds to the infinite possibilities of the universe, God had a better plan.

Now her heart is light, free, and clear on a spontaneous Sunday morning when she hadn't put on any make-up or made those earthy preparations for appearance. She found herself touched by God and fully understood that He loves us just the way we are.

Just As I Am!

I step out of the crowd
Just as I am;
And stand before God
And His glory.

No mask or disguise,
No pretense or shame,
As I open my heart
To His love.

Hardly an 'everyday miracle' was the realization that my children had grown up and were finding their own spiritual paths despite my perceived failure to provide them with an acceptable religious upbringing. Confusion about my own faith left me a poor example in this area, and guilt was a natural reaction for someone with a hell-fire and brimstone religious background.

Is it possible my guilt was unnecessary? Which is worse, feeling guilty for not providing the right influence? Or realizing what I did or didn't do might not be as earth-shattering as I first thought? If I am responsible only for my choices and my adult children are responsible for theirs, maybe I can accept all of us as 'works in progress' and spend time enjoying the miracles happening in my life every day.

Everyday Miracles

Dwell not on the past,
For it is over.
Spend not today
Planning the future,
For it was never promised.

Rather, see the beauty
Of the blossom,
And experience the wonder
Of your own breath.

Don't miss God's
Everyday miracles,
For they are often
The best.

I was asked by a friend to write something of comfort as her daughter faced the necessity of aborting her pregnancy.

I wanted this to be poetry since that's what I do; however, the wise soul of this unborn child very clearly insisted this was a letter to Mom. We compromised and it evolved into both.

I learned no life is wasted or without purpose. This child never grew beyond a few weeks in the womb but its message and impact have been profound and meaningful for many people.

This soul completed its mission in this life, and it is my great pleasure to introduce you to The Pea . . .

The Pea

I am just a tiny thing,
Much smaller than a pea.
But even so I feel your love
Surround the very core of me.

Though my life on earth was brief,
It wasn't without purpose.
For I was sent to bring you hope
And reaffirm your worth.

So always remember . . . I chose you.
And even in the choosing
I knew the path . . . its length and breadth;
And gladly made the journey.

In the land from whence I come, lives are not measured in days, weeks or years, but rather in the amount of love exchanged. Even though we never sang or rocked or laughed together, I bring you God's love and His promise of a healing time ahead. I have felt your love in your pain of letting go.

So grieve for the experiences we'll never share and cry the tears of loss, but never blame or second guess yourself; for remember . . . I chose you! And even in the choosing, I knew the path . . . its length and breadth . . . and still I chose to come. I needed to share your special brand of love and in that I have succeeded!

Unborn . . . But Not Unloved

Possibilities

My babies are all grown up.
There is no one left to nurture.

Who am I now?
What will I do?

There are no more birdies
To teach to fly.
No more ouchies to kiss
Or hurts to mend.

Who am I now?

For most of my life I've been a Mom,
And suddenly I'm just me.
Who am I now?
Or maybe I should ask,
Who would I like to be?

Part III

Adventures
With
God

Each morning I ask . . .

"What must I do today to be true to myself?"

The answer becomes my first priority, for to do anything else is to deny the rest of the day my full potential.

Dedicated to my friend, Carolyn, whom I admire for many things but especially for her courage in being willing to "fly" through her fears.

Angel of God

The Angel of God goes with you.
She follows wherever you lead.
When you are folded
Safe in Her arms of love,
Your journey will surely succeed.

I was in bed with a severe case of strep throat the day I wrote this, and I didn't realize the significant role it would later play in my life. It made me angry at the time. Thanks, God, for the STREP . . . I don't think so!

Later I realized that day was the first time in a long time I had given myself permission to simply rest. Permission to take a time-out from a very busy life. It had taken a strep infection to get my attention and allow me to rest my body. It was actually a perfect day and that realization has allowed me over the years to get through other "perfect days" in order to see the miracle imbedded in what often felt like a painful experience.

This prayer of gratitude pops into my head many mornings when I awaken, and I always know there is an adventure on the horizon.

A Perfect Day

Thank you, Lord
For a Perfect Day,
A perfect day in every way.

Guided by your loving hand
I'll use this day the best I can.

Thank you, Lord
For a Perfect Day.
Perfect for me in every way.

I include this poem as a personal indulgence in hopes that an unidentified young woman will see it and know how much I appreciated her kindness. My first time snorkeling was a very frightening but exhilarating experience for me. There was no rational reason to be frightened since I was wearing a life jacket and a ski belt as well as holding tightly onto a boogie board. Shamu himself could not easily have drowned me, but my lifelong fear of the water was powerful. I was anxious but resolved to get a glimpse of the world below the surface of the sea off the shore of Maui.

A young woman on the same excursion left her family to swim to me and ask if I would like to see the sea turtles. A thrill ran through my body like lightning. "Oh, yes. I would love to see the turtles!" She took my hand and swam with me to an area where I watched in awe as those beautiful and graceful turtles swam freely below us.

I was never sure I had properly thanked her or communicated how much it meant to me. I do not know her name and I never saw her again. She was my angel that day, and I smile whenever I remember her kindness.

- June 1996 -

Feel the love of a stranger
And you have felt the love of God.

She reached out her hand to me,
A simple gesture of love;
Offering to show me the way
To glimpse things not seen from above.

I saw another world
Beneath the rolling seas.
I saw amazing creatures
Created by God for me.
I appreciate the beautiful fish
The graceful, gentle turtles.
But I am ever grateful for the love of a stranger
Who went out of her way that day.

In Search of Beauty

Beauty isn't always found in soft,
    comfortable places.
It often thrives in the midst of the most
    intimidating thorns.
Only those brave enough to risk the hurt
Breathe the sweet nectar of the miracle.

If you find yourself in the middle of a
    prickly situation
Be still, take a deep breath and look around.
There is a miracle waiting to be recognized.

Thank you, God, for healing my fear of storms.

Thank you for replacing that fear with a love and appreciation of the rain, thunder, and lightning. I celebrate Your love and power everytime I hear the rolling thunder or rain beating down.

Thank you for loving me and helping me realize my love for You.

Storms

The thunder rolls across my soul
Like a mother's tender embrace.
And the soft gentle rain fills my spirit
With the joy of love overflowing.

The lightning flashes, bright and bold,
And I am again reminded of God's infinite power.
I rest . . . content and at peace,
Surrounded by the security of God's love.

In retrospect I feel I've written some powerful things in my car, in the rain, traveling up and down the freeways. On this particular morning I was on my way to work and the rainstorm was intense, causing traffic to slow to a crawl.

I turned off the radio and listened to the sound of the raindrops pounding on the car and appreciated the power contained in the combining of the individual droplets. The twenty-five mile journey to work took an hour and a half. I enjoyed the watery concert and chose not to allow the stress of the delay to infect my mood.

It was a very productive morning!

Raindrops

We all know the power of the thunderbolt
And lightning flashes,
But seldom appreciate the power of a single
raindrop.
The raindrop is a tiny, harmless thing.
Added one to the other and left unattended
They grow and swell to mighty rivers,
Overflowing their banks.

Tend to the raindrops that come along in your life,
Don't wait for them to become fearful and
complex.

We must call on God for guidance
In every aspect of life,
Not just at times when our problems threaten
To sweep us away.
For if we are holding God's hand
And celebrating his love,
The thunderbolts and lightning flashes
Become opportunities, miracles of growth
For us to appreciate.

I woke early on this cold, rainy Saturday morning apparently just so I could appreciate the blessing of sharing my bed with a warm body. I woke with the words of this piece sliding through my mind like a ribbon until I got up to write them down.

How many mornings have I awakened to this blessing and not fully appreciated it? My husband, Tom, and I have been married over 50 years and slept apart only a fraction of those days; so do the math if you like . . . it's enough for me to realize it's a lot of warm, cozy mornings.

I love this man, and not just because he's willing to share his warmth when I'm cold, but for all the love and support he's given me throughout our life together.

For that and so much more, I am grateful.

- Saturday, 6:44am -

I lie awake
In the darkness
Listening
To the rain.

It is neither morning
Nor nighttime,
But the gentle, sweet
Inbetween time of awakening.

I feel the stirring
Of the warmth beside me;
Comfort and security,
Solid, my Touchstone.

All is well.
I am at peace;
I drift back to sleep
To the gentle rhythm of the rain.

I enjoy the beach. Walking or just sitting on the sand watching the waves and listening to the symphony of sounds rejuvenates me. I was doing just that recently while writing in my journal and enjoying the day when I was approached by an older woman who was taking a casual stroll down the beach.

She had been watching me and had decided that maybe I was writing a book or a story and she was curious enough to ask. We talked for a few minutes and she shared with me that she and her husband had been coming to this beach for many, many years before his death two years ago. She laughed and said she felt like he had come along with her this time rather than being left back at home where he was buried. She could feel his closeness and remarked about how much joy he had brought her with his luck at finding treasures in the sand.

After she left I jotted down this poem and hurriedly copied it into a legible format with the intention of sharing it with her on her return. However, I did not see her again although I returned to the beach several mornings.

*I guess she was right. I **was** writing a story . . . about life and the timeless quality of love that is shared with another. I hope she reads this someday and recognizes her story and comes to know what an inspiration she was to me that day.*

Companions

Today I felt your presence
Walking peacefully beside me;
Enjoying the places and experiences
We shared in the past.

I miss your touch,
Your physical presence,
Your laughing face,
Your joy of discovery.

I am ever grateful
For our love,
Daily echoing my footsteps
Even now when you are gone.

It frightens me to write about Alzheimers because I fear the lesson in this piece for myself. There is always a lesson for me even when I write something that is inspired by events and people outside my own personal experiences. I've read poems years after writing them, only then realizing the importance of the message in my own life.

Recently it seems everyone I meet and talk to is dealing with this disease . . . some on a direct, personal level and others as a frightening future potential. The common theme among those dealing with a loved one stricken by Alzheimers is the tenacity of the brain in its attempt to hold onto each bit of information even as recognition slips into the abyss.

It is, however, not a battle of determination and strength. It is the quiet succumbing to a silent invader. Often the eyes of the caretaker are the only safety point.

In Your Eyes

This evil disease is a robber
Of time – of memory – of self.
Outside your vision I am afraid
Of things I do not remember.

Today I exist only in your eyes;
You remember who I really am.
Sadly, I do not.

The past no longer exists;
A future is unimaginable.
There is only this moment
When I recognize safety in your eyes.

I embrace this precious gift of the present
With the desperation of one
Who knows nothing else.

I believe the dead are not lost to us. Their energy and essence surrounds us . . . ready and willing to offer support and comfort in times of great need. Silence of mind and an open heart are key ingredients to this awareness.

I grieve today with my cousin who quickly and unexpectedly lost her husband yesterday. His physical presence is lost to her and their family, and the grief is overwhelming. I pray his memory and spirit will bring her the comfort and reassurance she needs to get through this time.

Awakening

I am with you
As I've always been
And always will be.

Open your heart
Quiet your mind
To feel my presence.

For I am with you
And simply await
Your awakening.

We've all seen them alongside the roads and freeways . . . those small white crosses placed where a loved one died, decorated with flowers and assorted remembrances. I notice them everytime we travel to the beach along the twisting, winding road from Columbus, Georgia to Eufaula, Alabama. I wonder about the circumstances of each life and death, and I mentally pause to feel grateful for my life and its many blessings.

The crosses seem to call out "someone loved me enough to place this here" and I know that person also holds cherished memories that are the real monument to the lost loved one . . . a monument that will endure when all the others have faded away.

I wrote the first four lines of this piece over a month ago and have struggled to find the words to complete it. The unexpected death of my cousin's husband yesterday pulled this piece immediately into my consciousness and I knew what the "rest of the story" should be. Thank you, Richard. I have learned simply to write down what I'm given and wait patiently on completion.

In Loving Memory

You need not mark the place
Where I left this world;
Nor the place where
My body lies resting.

The essence of my life
Will endure through time
In memories of love
Etched forever on our souls.

I drove home from work late one December evening in a pouring rain that slashed across the highway making progress slow at best and impossible at times. I was suddenly overcome with an intense sadness that brought tears to my eyes as the first few words of this poem began to manifest in my mind. After fumbling around for a pen and paper I realized I had to stop and write the words rolling through my mind. I exited the freeway, found a parking lot and hastily jotted these words onto a blank page in my daily planner. And I cried!

In the warm cocoon of my car I read what I had written and wondered if it was a message for my family . . . was I about to die? As quickly as the frightening thought popped into my mind, the answer followed. What I had written was for a cousin whose husband at that time was dying of cancer. He waged a long and valiant fight with a disease that ultimately took his life, and I finally shared this with his wife several weeks after his death. It was a message she told me she needed to hear and I was honored Spirit entrusted it to me.

Even though I'm personally in no hurry to deliver it to my family, I can think of no better message to leave behind.

Free

As you sit quietly and meditate on my life,
And remember the laughter and the love,
Even as you weep for the memories unborn,
Rejoice in your sorrow and pain.
The body before you
Is not me
For I am free.

I will soar with the eagles
And dance with the clouds.
My spirit has returned to a home of its own
And the flesh you return to the earth
Is not me
For I am free.

And so are you . . .

When I wrote this piece I was commuting every day on one of Atlanta's busiest freeways to and from my job in 'Corporate America'. I often found myself in gridlocked traffic moving forward slowly by inches. Many times I watched the frustration of other drivers, and often experienced that helpless, panicked, why-isn't-this-moving-faster feeling myself.

It was on one of these mornings when I happened to notice the butterfly enjoying the wildflowers at the edge of the freeway. Truly, I had never even been aware of the flowers before and I realized that I was often moving too fast in my life. I sometimes failed to see the beauty lying right at my feet.

I watched this graceful creature for several minutes and even felt sad when the pace of the traffic picked up, moving me beyond his range. But the butterfly's message always finds me whenever I allow myself to become too caught up in the chaos of daily living and I'm reminded to enjoy the banquet of beauty God has provided.

The Butterfly

There is a universe
Outside our chaos,
Outside the hustle and hurry,
Outside the work and worry.

Alongside the freeways
We travel so fiercely,
A small black butterfly
Floats from flower to flower,
Simply enjoying the nectar.
Never once wondering
If there will be enough.

Just once in awhile,
Stop and be the butterfly.
Drink deeply of today's nectar,
And embrace the joy
Of simply being.

My life has been a journey, a wonderful adventure during which I haven't always appreciated the different phases along the way. I have often blamed myself or circumstances and was anxious to just get through it rather than recognizing the lessons offered in each chapter.

I've come to understand that the journey is more important than the destination or goal. Each step must be seen as precious and necessary. All are simply pieces of a life in the process of transformation, change, growth, the very thing that adds richness to this human experience and makes it so precious.

I want to savour all the stages of the transformation realizing that each supports me in ways the next one cannot.

Becoming the Butterfly

When I was simply an egg
I was pure potential; anticipation.
I dreamed always of my goal
Of being the butterfly.

Becoming a caterpillar
Felt heavy, slow and cumbersome.
I railed at the pace and blamed myself
As I longed to be the butterfly.

Wrapped finally in my cocoon
I felt safe and secure;
But failed to appreciate this serenity
In anticipation of being the butterfly.

Now at this time of rebirth
I cling tenaciously to the umbilical cord.
As my wings dry and I prepare for flight
I question my haste in getting here.

Am I finally the butterfly?
Will my wings lift me up,
Or will I fall to my death?
I realize I cannot know for sure.

I must let go of the cord,
Spread my wings
Give in to the unseen currents of the wind
And embrace this new adventure.

Journey of a Dream

The journey of a dream
Begins as a tiny, fragile hope
For what seems impossible to achieve.
A ghost of a thought, imaginings.
Could it be possible? Dare I believe?

Doubt becomes a nagging companion
To be soothed and supplicated.
Small victories sustain forward motion.
Strength is gained with obstacles overcome.
It might be possible. I want to believe!

Destination in sight; I wait breathless.
Anxious to arrive at my goal,
To hold the precious dream
To own the brilliance of accomplishment!
Possibility becomes reality!

Wrapped in the abundance of celebration
A tentative light emerges on the horizon,
Illuminating the promise of a new dream.
It beckons me forward, testing my resolve.
And I leap, ready for the next adventure,
For now, as never before,
I trust in the journey of the dream!

From the author...

The pathways of faith are as varied as the leaves on the trees or the grains of sand on the beach. I hope you will choose the path that is yours and enjoy the blessings while being open to the lessons learned from the challenges presented.

May God bless you and keep you safe in His arms as you travel the path you have chosen.

Darlene Carter

Index

Index

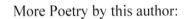

More Poetry by this author:

My Heart to Yours

available at
Amazon.com
www.JourneyofaDream.com

Made in the USA
Lexington, KY
10 December 2019

58354700R00061